ILLINOIS

The Prairie State

BY
JOHN HAMILTON

Abdo & Daughters

An imprint of Abdo Publishing | abdopublishing.com

abdopublishing.com

Published by ABDO Publishing, a division of ABDO, PO Box 398166, Minneapolis, Minnesota 55439. Copyright © 2017 by Abdo Consulting Group, Inc. International copyrights reserved in all countries. No part of this book may be reproduced in any form without written permission from the publisher. ABDO & Daughters™ is a trademark and logo of ABDO Publishing.

Printed in the United States of America, North Mankato, Minnesota.
012016
092016

Editor: Sue Hamilton   **Contributing Editor:** Bridget O'Brien
Graphic Design: Sue Hamilton
Cover Art Direction: Candice Keimig   **Cover Photo Selection:** Neil Klinepier
Cover Photo: iStock
Interior Images: Alamy, AP, Chicago Bears, Chicago Blackhawks, Chicago Bulls, Chicago Cubs, Chicago Fire, Chicago Sky, Chicago White Sox, Corbis, Dairy Queen International, Getty, Glow, Granger, Gunter Kuchler, History in Full Color-Restoration/Colorization, Howard Pyle, iStock, John Deere, Library of Congress, McDonald's, Morton Pumpkin Festival, Mile High Maps, & U.S. Federal Government.

Statistics: *State and City Populations*, U.S. Census Bureau, July 1, 2014 estimates; *Land and Water Area*, U.S. Census Bureau, 2010 Census, MAF/TIGER database; *State Temperature Extremes*, NOAA National Climatic Data Center; *Climatology and Average Annual Precipitation*, NOAA National Climatic Data Center, 1980-2015 statewide averages; *State Highest and Lowest Points*, NOAA National Geodetic Survey.

Websites: To learn more about the United States, visit booklinks.abdopublishing.com. These links are routinely monitored and updated to provide the most current information available.

Cataloging-in-Publication Data

Names: Hamilton, John, 1959- author.
Title: Illinois / by John Hamilton.
Description: Minneapolis, MN : Abdo Publishing, [2017] | Series: The United
    States of America | Includes index.
Identifiers: LCCN 2015957602 | ISBN 9781680783155 (lib. bdg.) |
    ISBN 9781680774191 (ebook)
Subjects: LCSH: Illinois--Juvenile literature.
Classification: DDC 977.3--dc23
LC record available at http://lccn.loc.gov/2015957602

CONTENTS

THE PRAIRIE STATE

Illinois is a state with its feet planted firmly in the soil of America's Midwest. In the south, fields of corn and soybeans stretch to the horizon, lending the state its nickname: The Prairie State. In the north, bustling cities are home to millions. Chicago is the busiest city of all. More than half of all Illinois residents live in the "Windy City" or its suburbs, drawn to its skyscrapers, blues and jazz clubs, Lake Michigan, and deep-dish pizza.

Illinois is a state on the go. It is a center of transportation. Much of what the Midwest region produces passes through Illinois, either on railroads, trucks, ships, or airplanes.

The Illinois state capital is Springfield. It was here that the state's most famous resident, President Abraham Lincoln, made his home. That is why Illinois is often called the "Land of Lincoln."

Vast fields of corn and soybeans spread across Illinois.

An early-morning view of the Chicago skyline from Lake Michigan.

QUICK FACTS

ILLINOIS

Name: Illinois got its name from the French spelling of a Native American group of tribes called the Illiniwek.

State Capital: Springfield, population 116,809

Date of Statehood: December 3, 1818 (21st state)

Population: 12,880,580 (5th-most populous state)

Area (Total Land and Water): 57,914 square miles (149,997 sq km), 25th-largest state

Largest City: Chicago, population 2,722,389

Nicknames: The Prairie State; Land of Lincoln

Motto: State Sovereignty, National Union

State Bird: Cardinal

State Flower: Violet

State Mineral: Fluorite

State Tree: White Oak

State Song: "Illinois"

Highest Point: Charles Mound, 1,235 feet (376 m)

Lowest Point: 279 feet (85 m), on the Mississippi River

Average July High Temperature: 86°F (30°C)

Record High Temperature: 117°F (47°C), in East St. Louis on July 14, 1954

Average January Low Temperature: 18°F (-8°C)

Record Low Temperature: -36°F (-38°C), in Congerville on January 5, 1999

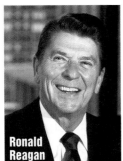

Average Annual Precipitation: 40 inches (102 cm)

Number of U.S. Senators: 2

Number of U.S. Representatives: 18

U.S. Presidents Born in Illinois: Ronald Reagan

U.S. Postal Service Abbreviation: IL

 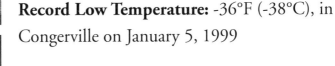

GEOGRAPHY

Illinois is the 25th-largest state of the United States. It covers 57,914 square miles (149,997 sq km) of land. Much of the land is flat, or gently rolling hills.

Illinois shares borders with Iowa and Missouri to the west. To the north lies Wisconsin. Kentucky is to the south, and to the east is Indiana.

Thousands of years ago, glaciers covered most of Illinois, except for a small part of the extreme southern tip. The glaciers scoured the land and flattened it. After they melted, they left behind huge areas of grasslands. The grasses grew and died for many centuries, creating rich soil. Today, most of Illinois grassland prairies have been converted to farmland.

Illinois is called "The Prairie State."

Illinois's total land and water area is 57,914 square miles (149,997 sq km). It is the 25th-largest state. The state capital is Springfield.

Illinois measures 378 miles (608 km) from north to south. But measured at its widest point, it is only 212 miles (341 km) east to west. Much of its western and eastern borders are formed by the meandering Mississippi, Ohio, and Wabash Rivers.

The state's midsection is called the "Heart of Illinois." Large, flat farm fields filled with corn and soybeans seem to be everywhere. Small towns and some larger cities are scattered across the central plains.

The northeast corner of Illinois is sometimes nicknamed Chicagoland. It is dominated by the city of Chicago, its suburbs, and other large urban areas.

Chicago is called "The City on the Prairie.

The extreme southern part of Illinois was left untouched by glaciers during the last Ice Age. There are more hills and forests here. Shawnee National Forest is in this part of the state.

The highest spot in Illinois is in the extreme northwest part of the state. Charles Mound rises 1,235 feet (376 m) above sea level. The state's lowest elevation is on the Mississippi River in the south, at just 279 feet (85 m) above sea level.

For shipping goods, the state's most important river is the Mississippi River. It forms the western border of Illinois. Other rivers include the Wabash, Ohio, Chicago, Kankakee, Calumet, and Illinois Rivers. The state's largest inland body of water is man-made Carlyle Lake. Lake Michigan borders the state's northeastern corner.

CLIMATE AND
WEATHER

Illinois is situated in the north-central part of the United States, which means it mainly has a humid continental climate. Because the state is almost 400 miles (644 km) long from north to south, there are some variations in climate. In general, Illinois has hot summers and cold, snowy winters. The southern part of the state is usually warmer in winter, with less snow.

Commuters walk through a snowy Chicago train station in February.

In July, the average high temperature is 86°F (30°C). The hottest temperature ever recorded in Illinois was on July 14, 1954, when the thermometer soared to 117°F (47°C) in East St. Louis. In January, the average low temperature is 18°F (-8°C). On January 5, 1999, the temperature sank to a record low of -36°F (-38°C) in the town of Congerville.

An August thunderstorm brings rain, thunder, and lightning to Alton, Illinois.

Statewide, Illinois receives an annual average of 40 inches (102 cm) of precipitation. In the summer, there are frequent thunderstorms, which can include hail or tornadoes. In the winter, blizzards can sometimes strike.

CLIMATE AND WEATHER

PLANTS AND
ANIMALS

There are more than 250 tree species in Illinois. About 70 are native to the state. Most of the original forests of Illinois were cut down long ago to make room for farm fields and for use as firewood and for building materials. More than 190,000 acres (76,890 ha) of little-used farmland have been replanted with trees since 1991, thanks to conservation programs. Oak and hickory make up about 53 percent of Illinois forests. Elm, ash, and cottonwood account for 22 percent. Other trees include pine, gum, maple, beech, willow, and cypress. White oak is the official state tree. It is prized for its strong and long-lasting wood.

White Oak is the
Illinois state tree.

Blue Spiderworts

Shooting Stars

Violets

   Illinois has dozens of native wildflower species. They come in many shapes and colors. Some are found in shady, wooded areas, while others bloom in open prairies and fields. Illinois wildflowers include spiderwort, shooting star, bluebell, coneflower, daisy, aster, goldenrod, lilac, morning glory, prairie rose, sunflower, and lily. The official state flower of Illinois is the violet. It has delicate purple petals and a long growing season.

Deer

The official state animal of Illinois is the white-tailed deer. It is the only native species of deer in the state. An adult male (buck) deer can weigh up to 250 pounds (113 kg). Other plentiful mammals in Illinois include shrews, skunks, chipmunks, gophers, opossums, raccoons, muskrats, weasels, rabbits, squirrels, mice, beavers, bats, badgers, minks, bobcats, foxes, moles, voles, coyotes, and river otters. In recent years, armadillos have been spotted in southern Illinois.

Male Cardinal

Female Cardinal

Millions of birds inhabit forests, fields, and wetlands in Illinois. Some are permanent residents, while others migrate when the seasons change. Common birds seen in the state include bluebirds, larks, bobwhites, woodpeckers, magpies, chickadees, wrens, finches, goshawks, owls, golden eagles, plovers, seagulls, pelicans, herons, sandpipers, terns, loons, and grebes. The official state bird of Illinois is the cardinal. The male has a bright-red coloring and a loud, whistling song. It is a yearlong resident of the state.

Illinois has many species of fish in its inland lakes, rivers, and streams. Lake Michigan is also an important fish habitat. Fish found swimming in Illinois waters include crappies, carp, catfish, salmon, gar, darter, perch, paddlefish, shiner, herring, and bowfin. The official Illinois state fish is the bluegill. This medium-sized panfish is a member of the sunfish family.

Bluegill

PLANTS AND ANIMALS

HISTORY

The ancestors of modern Native Americans (called Paleo-Indians) first arrived in the Illinois area about 10,000 years ago. Around 700 AD, one group began building a large settlement called Cahokia near present-day Collinsville, in

Paleo-Indians hunted large mammals such as woolly mammoths in Illinois.

southwestern Illinois. It grew big enough to house up to 20,000 residents. These Mississippian Culture people built hundreds of earthen mounds used in religious ceremonies. Pyramid-like Monks Mound is the largest earthen structure ever built in North America. Made of soil and clay, it is about 100 feet (30 m) high, 955 feet (291 m) long, and 775 feet (236 m) wide. At its base, it is about the same size as Egypt's Great Pyramid of Giza.

The Mississippian Culture disappeared from Illinois about 600 years ago. Nobody knows exactly why. They may have been forced to move because they used up the area's resources, or war with neighboring people might have wiped them out.

In the 1500s, a group of Native American tribes came together and formed the Illiniwek (or Illinois) Confederacy. Then, in the late 1600s, the area was invaded by Algonquian-speaking Native Americans—many of them Iroquois—from the east, forcing out most of the Illiniwek.

Monks Mound is the largest earthen structure ever built in North America. It is located near Collinsville, Illinois. Visitors can walk up concrete stairs to the top.

In 1673, French-Canadian explorer and fur trader Louis Jolliet and French missionary Father Jacques Marquette explored Illinois, travelling down the Mississippi River.

The first Europeans to explore Illinois were Father Jacques Marquette, a French missionary, and French-Canadian explorer and fur trader Louis Jolliet. In 1673, Marquette and Jolliet led an expedition by canoe down the Mississippi River. They traveled the length of modern-day Illinois's western border. Marquette spoke Native American languages, so he learned much from the tribes they encountered. After traveling farther down the Mississippi River, they finally turned back. On their return journey, they paddled up the Illinois River. The expedition ended near the site of modern-day Chicago. Their journey led to further explorations and France claiming the land.

Within a few years, more French explorers entered Illinois. In 1680, a fort was constructed near the modern-day city of Peoria. Small French settlements began to appear.

In 1754, Great Britain and France started a conflict called the French and Indian War. Nine years later, France lost. It handed over its lands east of the Mississippi River, including Illinois, to Great Britain.

In 1775, the United States began fighting the American Revolution. When it won the war for independence from Great Britain in 1783, it also gained huge amounts of land called the Northwest Territory. It included the future states of Illinois, Ohio, Indiana, Michigan, Wisconsin, and part of Minnesota.

Illinois Territory was formed in 1809. Just nine years later, on December 3, 1818, Illinois became the 21st state admitted to the Union.

In February 1779, Colonel George Rogers Clark led a military force of about 170 American and French frontiersmen across the Illinois countryside. Clark's frigid 18-day journey resulted in his American forces retaking the British-held Fort Sackville in neighboring Vincennes, Indiana.

Barges loaded with grain from Chicago are towed across Lake Michigan, headed for the Erie Canal.

The Erie Canal opened in 1825 in New York. This made it possible for Illinois farmers to quickly ship grains from Chicago across the Great Lakes to big eastern markets like New York City. Starting in the 1840s, railroads began connecting Chicago to points all over the Midwest. Barge traffic increased on the Mississippi and Ohio Rivers and other waterways. Illinois became an important transportation hub for goods shipped all over the country. This made the area very attractive to new businesses. The state's population boomed. By 1860, more than 100,000 people lived in Chicago alone.

In 1860, Illinois-native Abraham Lincoln was elected president of the United States. He vowed to end the evil practice of slavery. His election led 11 Southern states to leave the Union. The Civil War (1861-1865) soon gripped the country. More than 250,000 Illinois soldiers fought to keep the Union together. Under Lincoln's leadership, the war ended in 1865 and the slaves were freed.

After the Civil War, Illinois began to rapidly industrialize. Even more railroads were built. Growth continued over the following decades. The northern third of Illinois, especially the Chicago area, became very urbanized. In 1955, Chicago's busy O'Hare International Airport began commercial flights. In 1959, the opening of the St. Lawrence Seaway gave Illinois direct access through the Great Lakes to the Atlantic Ocean and ports around the world. Today, Illinois continues to be an economic powerhouse.

Illinois-native Abraham Lincoln was elected president of the United States in 1860.

DID YOU KNOW?

• On the night of October 8, 1871, a fire in downtown Chicago killed more than 200 people, left 75,000 homeless, and burned most of the city's business district. The Great Chicago Fire started in a shed next to a barn. Some think a cow kicked over a lantern. Despite the devastation, Chicago was quickly rebuilt.

• The first McDonald's restaurant opened on April 15, 1955, in the city of Des Plaines, Illinois, near Chicago. Fifteen years earlier, on June 22, 1940, the first Dairy Queen opened in the city of Joliet. Soft-serve ice cream cones were sold for five and ten cents. The building still stands in Joliet, and is recognized as a landmark.

• From 1920 until 1933, the sale and production of alcoholic drinks was outlawed. Called Prohibition, it led to organized crime gangs selling liquor illegally. One of the most violent Chicago gangs was led by Al Capone. After years of evading the law, he was finally convicted in 1931 and sent to prison—for failing to pay his taxes.

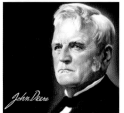

- When new farmers first settled Illinois, they had to first plow the thick prairie sod so they could plant seeds. Most plows were made of cast iron, which the sticky soil clung to and had to be cleaned off every few steps. In 1837, John Deere, of Grand Detour, Illinois, invented the self-scouring steel plow. It was shaped so that the soil fell away as the furrows were cut. Deere sold thousands of plows to grateful farmers. The invention revolutionized agriculture and helped many farmers settle the land.

- Morton, Illinois, is the self-proclaimed "Pumpkin Capital of the World." This small central-Illinois town holds the Morton Pumpkin Festival each year to celebrate the fall pumpkin harvest. More than 70,000 visitors come from all over the state to enjoy the festival. It features a 10k race, a craft fair, a parade, and a pumpkin pie eating contest. More than 80 percent of the world's canned pumpkins are processed at Morton's Nestlé canning plant.

- The tallest man in history was Robert Wadlow (1918-1940). He was from Alton, Illinois. According to the Guinness Book of World Records, he officially stood 8 feet, 11.1 inches (2.7 m) tall, and weighed 492 pounds (223 kg). He wore a size 37AA shoe, and his arm span was more than 9.5 feet (2.9 m).

PEOPLE

Abraham Lincoln (1809-1865) was the 16th president of the United States. Lincoln was intelligent and compassionate. Born in Kentucky in 1809, he moved with his family first to Indiana, and then to Illinois, where he finally settled. Mostly self-educated, he became a lawyer in 1836. After several years in state

politics, the people of Illinois elected him to the United States House of Representatives in Washington, DC. In March 1861, after winning election as an anti-slavery Republican, Lincoln took office as president of the United States, just as the country was plunged into its greatest crisis—the Civil War. Through Lincoln's guidance, the Union won the war in 1865. However, Lincoln was killed by an assassin's bullet that same year.

Barack Obama (1961-) served as the 44th president—and first African American president—of the United States. He was born in Hawaii, but moved to Illinois after graduating from New York's Columbia University. After graduating from Harvard Law School in Massachusetts, he returned to Illinois. He was elected to the U.S. Senate in 2004, and then was elected two terms as U.S. president, serving as a Democrat from 2009 to 2017.

Ronald Reagan (1911-2004) was the 40th president of the United States, serving from 1981 to 1989. He was born in Tampico, in northern Illinois. He was a famous Hollywood actor during the 1930s, 1940s, and 1950s. Starting in 1967, he served eight years as California's governor before being elected president in 1980. As a Republican president, his goal was to limit government and reduce taxes.

Hillary Rodham Clinton (1947-) was born in Chicago, Illinois. As a young woman growing up in the state, she became active in politics and public service. She married future President Bill Clinton in 1975. They met while both earned law degrees from Yale University. She spent 12 years in Arkansas as First Lady when Bill Clinton was governor of the state. During Bill Clinton's presidency, she served as the nation's First Lady in Washington, DC, from 1993 to 2001. She won election as a U.S. Senator from New York in 2000, serving from 2001 to 2009. She also served as President Barack Obama's Secretary of State from 2009 to 2013. In 2016, she became the first woman to run for president as a major political party candidate (Democrat).

James "Wild Bill" Hickok (1837-1876) was one of the most famous gunfighters of the Old West. He was born and raised near the tiny farming town of Homer, Illinois (called Troy Grove today). Hickok was a crack shot. He was a Union scout, lawman, express rider, and showman. In 1876, Hickok was killed in a saloon in Deadwood, Dakota Territory (today's South Dakota).

Oprah Winfrey (1954-) is one of the most popular talk-show hosts in the world. She was born in Mississippi, but relocated to Chicago, Illinois, to begin a career in television. Starting in 1986, *The Oprah Winfrey Show* aired more than 4,500 episodes over 25 seasons. Winfrey was also nominated for an Academy Award for her role in *The Color Purple*.

Jacqueline "Jackie" Joyner-Kersee (1962-) was born and raised in East St. Louis, Illinois. She competed as a track and field athlete in five Olympic Games in the 1980s and 1990s. She won two gold medals in the heptathlon event, plus a gold medal in the long jump. She also won a silver and two bronze medals. *Sports Illustrated* named her the greatest female athlete of the 20th century.

CITIES

Chicago is the most populous city in Illinois, and the third-most populous city in the entire country (behind New York City and Los Angeles). It has a population of 2,722,389. Together with its suburbs, it is home to almost 10 million people. Chicago was incorporated as a city in 1837. It grew quickly, thanks to its location near major rivers and Lake Michigan, which helped link the Midwest to markets in the eastern United States and Europe. Even today, half of all rail freight passes through the city. Today, Chicago is a center of business, education, science, entertainment, and politics. Some of the tallest buildings in the world are in Chicago, including the Willis Tower, which stands at 1,452 feet (443 m).

The city of **Rockford** is in north-central Illinois, on the banks of the Rock River. Rockford is the third-largest city in Illinois. Nicknamed the "Forest City," its population is 149,123. Manufacturing, transportation, and high-technology are important industries. Goods made in Rockford include furniture, farm implements, automobile parts, and aviation instruments.

Joliet is about 40 miles (64 km) southwest of Chicago in northern Illinois. Its population is 147,928. The city was incorporated in 1852 along the banks of the Des Plaines River, but began as a single log cabin almost 20 years earlier, in 1833. Today, Joliet's economy depends on manufacturing, medical care, and education. It is home to Chicagoland Speedway, which hosts NASCAR racing.

Springfield and the
Old State Capital

Lincoln's
Tomb

Abraham Lincoln
Presidential Library
and Museum

Springfield is the capital of Illinois. It is in central Illinois. Its population is
116,809. Before becoming president of the United States, Abraham Lincoln
made Springfield his home for almost 25 years. The president's tomb is
located in the city. Many Springfield residents earn their living working
for the state government. Other important industries include health care,
telecommunications, and education. The University of Illinois at Springfield
and Southern Illinois University School of Medicine are located in the city.
There are more than 30 parks in Springfield, including Washington Park
Botanical Garden. The Abraham Lincoln Presidential Library and Museum
is one of the most visited presidential libraries in the country.

Peoria Skyline

A Paddleboat on the Illinois River

A Bridge over the Illinois River

Peoria is in the heart of farm country, in the middle of Illinois. It was first settled by French explorers. They built a fort on the banks of the Illinois River in the late 1600s. In 1845, Peoria became an incorporated city. Today, about 115,828 people call Peoria home. Major industries include farm machinery, health care, education, factory maintenance, and information technology. Peoria is viewed as a typical "All-American City." Its motto is, "Will it play in Peoria?" That means that if a new product or service is liked by the citizens of Peoria, it will probably be liked all over America.

TRANSPORTATION

When it comes to transportation, Illinois is one of the most important states in the country. It has a central location in the Midwest, and a good system for moving people and products.

Most of the country's freight and passenger railroads connect in Illinois. There are approximately 9,982 miles (16,064 km) of railroad tracks in the state. Half of all freight passes through Chicago alone. The city is the single biggest rail hub in the nation.

Several major interstate highways crisscross Illinois, making it easier for passenger cars and trucks hauling freight to move around the state. Many roads lead into and out of the busy Chicago metro area. Illinois has about 145,708 miles (234,494 km) of public roadways.

New bridge overpasses are being built to handle Chicago's train traffic congestion.

Chicago O'Hare International Airport

Chicago's O'Hare International Airport is one of the busiest airports in the world. Illinois is also home to approximately 106 other public and private airports. More than 40 million passengers board commercial flights in Illinois each year.

There are 1,095 miles (1,762 km) of navigable waterways in Illinois. Ships and barges use these "water highways" to haul bulky freight such as heavy machinery, cement, coal, steel, and grain. About 116 million tons (105 million metric tons) of freight are hauled each year along Illinois waterways. Ships leaving Illinois can reach the Gulf of Mexico by traveling down the Mississippi, Illinois, and Ohio Rivers. Some ships reach the Atlantic Ocean by crossing Lake Michigan and connecting to the other Great Lakes.

Coal is transported down the Mississippi River.

NATURAL RESOURCES

The most important natural resource of Illinois is the state's rich soil. There are about 75,000 farms in Illinois, covering 27 million acres (10.9 million ha), which is about 75 percent of the state. Illinois ranks second in the nation (behind Iowa) in corn production. About half of the state's total farm income comes from raising corn. Soybeans, wheat, pigs, plus beef and dairy cows are also major farm products. Illinois exports many of its farm products to other states and countries. About 44 percent of Illinois grain is sold for export.

In the past 200 years, most of the forests of Illinois have been cut down to create farmland. Today, forestland makes up only about 12 percent of Illinois. That is approximately 4.4 million acres (1.8 million ha). Almost all of the trees in Illinois are hardwoods, such as white oak and black walnut. The state ranks 32nd in the nation for production of wood.

A coal mine in Carlinville, Illinois, loads tons of coal from its underground mining operation onto waiting train cars.

There are big deposits of coal under the ground of Illinois. Most of it is buried in the central and southern parts of the state. Small amounts of petroleum are found in southern Illinois. Other important mineral resources include industrial sand and gravel, plus crushed stone used in construction projects.

NATURAL RESOURCES

INDUSTRY

Illinois is a huge producer of manufactured goods. Most of the state's factories are located in the northeast, in or near Chicago. The most valuable category is machinery, such as construction equipment and machine tools. Chemicals are also very important to the Illinois economy. They are sold to companies all over the world to make products such as medicines, cosmetics, and foods. Other Illinois-manufactured goods include metal products, plastics, transportation equipment, and electronics. Food processing is also important.

The Caterpillar factory in Peoria, Illinois, builds huge construction and mining equipment. The factory opened in Peoria in 1910.

The Chicago Mercantile Exchange buys and sells contracts for huge amounts of commodities.

The part of the Illinois economy that brings in the most income is the services industry. It includes such businesses as banking, insurance, hotels, law firms, and real estate. Illinois is home to one of the nation's most important financial and commodity exchanges. A commodity is a raw material or farm product, such as corn, lumber, meat, cotton, energy, or gold. An exchange is a place where these basic resources are bought and sold in big quantities. Exchanges can also trade financial items such as interest rates and foreign money.

The Chicago Mercantile Exchange was founded in 1898. Customers buy and sell contracts for huge amounts of commodities. This helps set the price of the food we eat and the clothes we wear. Most trading today is done by computer by customers all over the world.

INDUSTRY

SPORTS

The Chicago area is home to several major league teams. Many have won world championships. Major League Baseball fans can root for the Chicago White Sox or the Chicago Cubs. The Cubs have played in the National League since its founding in 1876. Today, they play in famed Wrigley Field, one of the oldest ballparks in the country.

Wrigley Field was built in 1914. It is the second-oldest ballpark in Major League Baseball, after the 1912-built Fenway Park in Boston, Massachusetts. Wrigley Field can seat 41,160 fans.

Members of the Chicago Bears team carry off head coach Mike Ditka after defeating the New England Patriots in Super Bowl XX on January 26, 1986.

The Chicago Bears play for the National Football League. Their 1985-season Super Bowl win was led by legendary coach "Iron Mike" Ditka.

The Chicago Bulls dominated the National Basketball Association in the 1990s, thanks to Hall of Famers Michael Jordan and Scottie Pippen. The Chicago Sky plays for the Women's National Basketball Association.

The Chicago Blackhawks have been a powerhouse in the National Hockey League since their founding in 1926. As of 2015, they have taken home six Stanley Cup championships.

The Chicago Fire plays for Major League Soccer and has won several championships.

Illinois is also home to several minor league teams and college teams. Many of them are outside the Chicago area. The University of Illinois at Urbana-Champaign has several intercollegiate teams. Called the Fighting Illini, they are located in east-central Illinois. High school sports are also very popular in Illinois.

ENTERTAINMENT

Chicago's Loop District is the city's central downtown core. There are many exciting things to do within the bright lights of the Loop's historic borders. The Art Institute of Chicago is in Grant Park. It houses more than 300,000 pieces of artwork. The Chicago Symphony Orchestra, the Lyric Opera of Chicago, and the Joffrey Ballet are just three of the world-class music and dance venues found in the city. Chicago is famous for its blues and jazz nightclubs. There are also dozens of dance troupes, theatrical companies, comedy clubs, zoos, and art galleries.

Chicago's Millennium Park features the Cloud Gate sculpture. Commonly known as "The Bean," it is a popular tourist destination. Its mirror-like surface reflects the surrounding Chicago skyline.

The Field Museum's "Sue" is a *Tyrannosaurus rex* that is 42 feet (12.8 m) long.

Chicago's Field Museum is called a national treasure, thanks to its vast natural history collection. It includes Sue, the most complete fossil skeleton of a *Tyrannosaurus rex* ever found. The Museum of Science and Industry is the largest science museum in the Western Hemisphere. Exhibits include a replica coal mine, the Apollo 8 space capsule, and a captured World War II German submarine. The Shedd Aquarium is one of the largest aquariums in the world. It is home to more than 32,000 aquatic animals.

Shedd Aquarium

For outdoor lovers, Illinois has 72 state parks, 6 state forests, and 26 state wildlife areas. More than 44 million people visit Illinois state parks each year.

TIMELINE

1500s—Native Americans form the Illiniwek Confederacy.

1673—French explorers Father Jacques Marquette and fur trader Louis Jolliet enter Illinois.

Late 1600s—France begins to build forts and towns in Illinois.

1763—Great Britain controls Illinois.

1783—Britain surrenders Illinois to the United States.

1818—Illinois becomes the 21st state in the Union.

1820s—Illinois begins building canals.

1850s—Illinois becomes the Midwest's most important hub of transportation.

1861-65—Illinois fights in the Civil War on the side of its most famous citizen, President Abraham Lincoln.

1890s—Illinois becomes the biggest supplier of grains and beef to markets of the eastern United States.

1933—The World's Fair is held in Chicago.

1993—The Mississippi River floods many homes and businesses.

2009—Former Illinois Senator Barack Obama is sworn in as the 44th president of the United States.

2011—Oprah Winfrey tapes the final episode of *The Oprah Winfrey Show*. The daily talk show ran on network television for 25 seasons.

2015—The Chicago Blackhawks win the Stanley Cup championship.

2015—On October 12, the Cubs set a Major League playoff record by hitting six home runs against the St. Louis Cardinals in a single game.

TIMELINE

GLOSSARY

ACADEMY AWARD

An award presented to the year's best movie actors, writers, directors, producers, and technicians by the Academy of Motion Picture Arts and Sciences. It is also known as an Oscar, the gold statue awarded to the winners. About 40 Oscars are made each year by a manufacturer in Chicago, Illinois.

AMERICAN REVOLUTION

The war fought between the American colonies and Great Britain from 1775-1783. It is also known as the War of Independence and the Revolutionary War.

APOLLO SPACE PROGRAM

An American space exploration program that ran from 1963 to 1972. Run by the National Aeronautics and Space Administration (NASA), the program's goal was to land astronauts on the Moon and return them safely to Earth. The first Moon landing was achieved by Apollo 11 on July 20, 1969.

CANAL

A man-made river deep and wide enough for boat traffic. Canals are often shortcuts between cities or countries. People and cargo traveling on boats using canals can travel in less time than might otherwise be possible.

CIVIL WAR

The war fought between America's Northern and Southern states from 1861-1865. The Southern states were for slavery. They wanted to start their own country. Northern states fought against slavery and a division of the country.

Fur Trader

A person who buys and sells the soft, thick coat of hair taken from certain animals. The fur is later made into warm clothing. Beavers and minks are examples of animals from which the fur is taken.

Heptathlon

A track and field competition that combines seven events, including 100-meter hurdles, high jump, shot put, 200-meter sprint, long jump, javelin throw, and 800-meter run. Points are awarded for how well a competitor performs in each event. The three players with the highest number of combined points are awarded gold, silver, and bronze medals.

Industrialize

To change a society from one in which work is done mainly by hand to one in which work is done mainly by machines.

Midwest

A geographic region that occupies the north-central part of the United States. It is usually defined as including 12 states: Illinois, Indiana, Iowa, Kansas, Michigan, Minnesota, Missouri, Nebraska, North Dakota, Ohio, South Dakota, and Wisconsin.

NASCAR

National Association for Stock Car Auto Racing. A popular sporting event with races held across the United States.

Prairie

A large area of level or mostly level grassland.

Urban

Referring to a city or city life.

INDEX